KALEIDOSC

Asher Phoenix

The mind is a beautiful colorful space, but sometimes the voices of society try to turn it into a black and white tornado.

What you see and think isn't always the same as what others see or think.

So open that creative beautiful mind of yours, and try to color the world a little more vibrant!

Be different

*Be **brave***

*Love who want to **love***

*Have **courage***

*Have **strength***

And most of all

acways *be yourself*

Beautifully Shattered

"Welcome...Welcome...Welcome all to the great mirrors of the past & thoughts...So who wants to go first"

{{Silence}}

"You...you...you in the grey & purple snapback" pointed the announcer

I step towards the gangly tall guy with shaggy hair slowly.

"Five bucks please" demanded the gangly dude

I pulled out the money from my back pocket of my ripped jeans

Entering the nice spacious room full of mirrors. I looked around, and kept walking into the room. Then all of a sudden the room gets black as night. Looking around, feeling around. All I felt was mirrors, and then I felt something sharp on my finger.

Thinking...Fuck, what the hell

I grabbed for my phone, but it wasn't there. The dipshit must've pocketed me before I entered the room. I stuck my finger in my mouth and I tasted blood. I sighed as I started to get pissed. All of a sudden an old school song that I listened to back when I was younger came on....Hanson - Weird. Then a really dim light came on. I looked down and I saw droplets of blood on the cracked cement ground. I looked up, and all the mirrors were cracked, some pieces were missing. Looking all around, I couldn't find the fucking door I came in from.

The music stopped, and a voice came on the intercom

"Who are you?"

I kept looking around

"Let me outta here, what the fuck is this?" I yelled

"Who are you?"

"Why do you wanna know?" I asked

"Who are you?"

I walked up to the shattered mirror to see if there was an off switch or something. Then all of a sudden there were pictures of me when I was younger. I stood back, and looked at all of them. Me in casts, me in hospital beds, me in my leg braces. I smiled for a split second, and then I started to pick that little girl apart in my head.

"Who is that?" the voice asked

"It's me" I said

"What do you see?" asked the voice

"Why does it matter?" I said

"Who are you?" the voice asked

By this time I wanted to get the hell out of this hell hole. I started pounding on the shattered glass. My palms started to bleed, so I stopped. I just stood there looking at the shattered glass. Then more pictures came up, as Sara Bareilles - Brave started echoing off the walls. It was a picture of a pride flag casted over several pictures of me.

"Tell me...what is this?" the voice asked

"A pride flag" I said

"Ding...Ding...Ding" said the raspy voice

"Let me the fuck outta here" I yelled

"Who are you?" he asked again

I started to chuckle in anger, as I shook my head and licked my lips. Then I started to kick the shattered mirror. I told myself once I get the fuck out of here, I'm NEVER going into a fair ever again. I kicked the shattered mirror so hard that a medium piece fell out. I kept looking at it, then kicked it to the side. I bent down to look where the piece fell out, and it had concrete behind it.

Thinking...Fucking hell

I sat against the shattered mirror, and all of a sudden music came on. Kid Ink ft. MGK - Hell & Back (remix)blasted over the intercom. I looked around to see if I could see any cameras or speakers. Nothing in sight. Then for the third time pictures came up on the shattered mirror. A picture of my family, a picture of my best friend & I, and another picture of my other best friend and I, a picture of my black notebook & pen, and all my pieces I wrote. Then a mini clip of me doing a live reading my piece.

"What does this mean to you?"

"If I tell you will you let me go?" I yelled "It's everything & everybody I love" I said trying to hold back tears

"Who are you?"

"Why...why does it matter to you...why are asking me that" I asked playing with the piece of glass

"You are weak, a burden, worthless, you are disgusting because you like girls, you are crazy, you have no purpose....shall I go on" yelled the voice

I felt tears rolling down my warm cheeks. I felt defeated, tired. Then something clicked in my head, and then I started to get mad, fists hitting the cement. My knuckles started to turn red as I kept punching the cement. I screamed, and then I sat on the cold ground for a minute to collect my thoughts. I examined my knuckles, and tried not to get into my head.

"I know who I am" I yelled

"Then who are you?" asked the raspy voice

"I'm Ash...who is shattered...but...but I'm slowly picking up my pieces & putting them back together" I said picking at my palm

"Keep going..." the voice said

"I'm quirky, loving, caring, and sarcastic...I love to write...no...no I am a writer, and writing is my passion, always has been" I said

"Is that all..." asked the voice

"I'm fucking proud of who I am" I yelled wiping my tears away as I stood up

The lights turned off, and all the gaps in the shattered glass lit up in a fluorescent dark purple. I touched the glass, and a picture of me came up, with all the other pictures. Then lettering scrolled across

ALWAYS BELIEVE IN YOURSELF
ALWAYS BE TRUE TO YOURSELF

The room shook for about thirty seconds, and the mirror moved, and a door appeared. I looked around, collected myself, and then quickly walked out of the hallway. I saw the gangly tall dude smirking at me while taking the next person in line money.

"That's some fucked up shit man" I said as I walked

"Hey, Ash you forgot something"

I turned around and the gangly guy threw me a necklace. It was the piece of glass that fell out of the wall I kicked. The edges were very smooth with the fluorescent dark purple around the edges. I flipped it over, and engraved words on the back...

WRITER

"Thanks" I yelled as I put the necklace on

My Arthrogryposis Skeleton

Peel my chocolate skin away
And...
This skeleton was formulated
With weak muscles & different angles
You'll notice my left hip has screws and plates
You wouldn't know an estimate
Of how many surgeries I had
Unless you were an Anthropologist
Calling...
Temperance Brennan
I was conditioned & trained to adapt
In this world that wasn't built for this anatomy
The struggle was like a rollercoaster
But...
As the lone wolf
I worked hard to rise
And was taught to be as independent as I can be
If...
I fall down thinking I've lost the battle
I'll look my obstacle in the fucking eye
And rise above it
Like a gorgeous fierce phoenix
And I'll overcome it until
I burn that bitch down
With...
A don't fuck with me look on my face

Monroe's Love

(Dedicated To My Favorite Teacher & Best Friend)

She knew I was broken
Instead...
Of trying to fix me
She took the the time to understand me
She saw something inside that darkness
She wasn't scared of the rebel attitude
I would throw in her pathway
Because...
I always tried defending my territory
Before anyone could hunt me down
And hurt me first
She...
Loved me no matter how broken I was
She...
Never gave up on me
She...
Never walked away
She...
Called me out on my bullshit
She...
Disciplined me when needed
I did my time
And that was that
She...
Never threw my flaws in my face
And...
Always praised me whenever I did good

She...
Never raised her voice at me
And...
Always tried to explain things
In ways that I could understand
Apparently...
She saw something inside of me
Because...
She fucking loved me & my broken pieces
And...
I thank her for that

Automatic Ink Reload

Shit my pen is running low
Fuck it...I'm still writing this
Writing has always been easy for me
When I first started when I got grounded
Probably because I ran my attitude mouth
Or doing something stupid in school
Shit maybe both
Actually I guarantee it was both
All I know is that I wish
Falling fully in love with someone
Would be easy as writing
I wish trusting someone right off bat
Would be easy just like writing
It would be cool to defeat these demons
That lurk behind weak doors waiting for me
As I...
Stroke my pen as the ink bleeds
A magical spell that formulated
Onto the blank piece of paper
Then I'd light that motherfucker up
As I scream to the demons to leave
Wouldn't that be epic & easy just like writing
If my Mom was a notebook
And I was a pen
Speaking of pens...
I'm stretching the ink thin here
Sorry, where was I?
Then maybe...Just maybe

She would've understood ME a little bit more
And I wouldn't have been a rebel when I was younger
Ha...like Maury would say
"That's a lie"
Because...
I see this world as Black & White
With a mixture of tainted paint fragments
But...
When I write I see...
A kaleidoscope of beautiful vibrant colors
Dancing in my quirky mind
And...
You see writing is easy for me
Fuck my pen ran outta ink
Wait...
Click...Click...Click...Click
Automatic ink reload

Magical Spells

I'm craving your kisses
Every second of everyday
My hands wanting to wander
And caress your precious curves
Looking at the beautiful stars
Casting spells in the dark sky
Like Potter & Weasley
As we eat a box of Wheat Thins

Warriors Have Feelings Too

I wish that people would
Give a lot more credit to
People who aren't under the "normal" spectrum
Meaning...
The kid with Downs Syndrome
Who loves to draw
Let him be part of the art show
Or the girl that has Cerebral Palsy
Did you know that she has a mean 3 pointer
No...
Because you looked at her physical appearance
How about the teenage boy that has Epilepsy
All he wants to do is be on that tennis court
Or how about...
That cute little girl that has Autism
When music comes on
Oh my, she dances like an angel
She could be the next best ballerina
What about...
That boy that has anger problems
Maybe boxing would put his hands to use
And that girl who has Arthrogryposis Multiplex Congenita
Who always wanted to be a model
But gave that dream up because she saw on TV
That only people who walk right gets to do it
Fuck...fuck all that bullshit
Just because someone's armour is built differently
Doesn't mean theirs doesn't work

Give them a chance
And if they say you can't
Well my fellow team members
Coming from the Alphas month...
Stand up & **PROVE** them wrong
Because...
You are a fucking
WARRIOR

Lighthouse

You stand tall like a soldier ready for war
You work all year round, and never get tired
You get a beaten from whatever storm
Mother nature throws at you
You are built many different ways,
But…
Your job description never changes
You are a little girls flashlight
Someone's secret code
Between two people in love
You are someone's beacon of hope
For a fisherman lost at sea
You are a dance floor for angles
That dance on the clouds
You are the most important thing…
To people who are…
Lost, scared, trying to find their way home,
Or who are alone

You are a…

Lighthouse

Dear 12 Year Old Ash

I'm looking at you
And all I want to do is hug you
Because I know that you are drowning
In this huge tycoon that brewed up in your soul
Ash...Ash...
I know you are hiding your true self
Fighting your dark thoughts and mixed feelings
That's why you yell and wreak havoc
Because you want ONE person
JUST one person to understand, to care
But...
You are scared...you don't trust easily
Hey...Hey head up
I know you hate yourself
And feel alone...and dead inside
I get that no one will understand
And you think NO one will relate
Because...
People already judge you before knowing you
And stare at you because of your disability
I know you want to scream & cry
Listen...
You little badass
What I'm going to tell that no one ever told...
Well...you back then
That it's okay...it's okay
And there's many more like you
That it gets better

So...head up...snapback on...stand tall
Because...Ash it's okay
That you are gay

Ink In My Veins

It all started on a weekend
Of doing hard time...
Grounded
With a pen and a notebook that had like 30 pages
Across from me was my partner in crime...
My little brother
At the kitchen table
Time ticking slowly
Tick...Tock...Tick...Tock
Bored…
Opening the notebook...
I started to let my pen flow over the lined paper
One page
Five pages
Fifteen pages
I needed more paper after I filled the one I had
Something that was so fun & was also so easy
It was nothing I struggled with
I was proud of what I wrote
That's when I knew I loved to write
I wanted to be a writer

Dubstep Beat

When she dances
She ignites my soul
As the fire flames dances
To the dubstep beat
When she gets closer
I can feel that heat

Underdog Tags

I've always been an underdog
Since I took my first breath into the world
Not everyone is born an underdog
But...
The ones who are given that card
I think have the biggest hearts
But...
Also running away from demons
That others won't understand
Unless they walk a mile in my sneakers
My underdog tags...
Look vintage and worn down
But…
It also feels like courage and strength
If you run your fingers along it
I was born with a rare physical condition called
Arthrogryposis Multiplex Congentia
So I always had…
To adapt to a world that wasn't built for me
I always had to prove people who doubted me
My birth mother gave me up
So...
I'll always have those unanswered questions
- Does she think about me?
- Has she ever tried looking for me?
- I wonder if she's creative?
- Do I have her smile
Before...

My adoptive mother could adopt me
The system took me out of my perfect home
And put my well being in the hands of a monster
Apparently the system thought…
I'd be better off with a "black" mother
The monster only seen dollar signs on me
Instead of loving & protecting me
The monster damaged my trust & my soul
The system is fucking broken
And it'll always be fucking broken
I finally found my way back home
Where I belonged
Where I was loved
Where I was safe
Where I NEVER EVER had to feel cold
Where I could have unlimited cinnamon toast
Someone who I called Mom
Because...
She always smiled
Always sang me songs
Always made the best food
But...
Also someone who I loved
That had the same eye color as me
And always made sure I was WARM
So...
I've been an underdog my whole life
I might have sharp edges like a triangle
But...
Fuck....I wear my tags loud & proud

Rock Hunters

During the summertime my little brother & I would go rock hunting, and sometimes my other siblings would join in our quests as well.

My little brother and I would swim all around our lake property. We'd search for the best rocks,
Grey ones, pink ones with black dots, light green ones, black ones, smooth ones, jagged ones. Even ones with holes in them, or sometimes faces on them.

We would stick the buckets on our porch for later examinations. Our Mom would get so mad because we would have rocks everywhere.

One time we all went swimming to find two huge rocks so our Mon could make us Rock Soup. We thought it was the coolest recipe.

One time my brother got a hammer, told me to hold the rock so he could bust it open.

Wack....Wack...Wack

"OUCH"

Yeah that definitely was my damn finger.

There were two rocks I still remember til this day.
One was a really light teal rock, that had a faint black line in the middle. It had a hole in the center of it. So I made it into a necklace because I loved making jewelry. I pretend I made it for myself,

because well I was an asshole like that sometimes. Anyways, I seriously made it for my little brother. Then he lost it two days later.

The second rock was seriously magnificent. It was a faint white color, with dark tan markings outline of an Indian head...yes an Indian head. We gave it to our Mom, and she put it on the ledge above the sink.

If I could rewind time...this would be the memory I'd like to relive. It was one of many favorite memories and moments I had with my little brother.

Hospital Bracelets

Everyone has a story & their own hurdles
That they have to overcome or live with on a daily
I don't like to call it a disability or a struggle
It has a proper name
Arthrogryposis Multiplex Congentia
A name that majority of people who say it
Say it wrong more than once
But....
Shit I had a hard time saying it when I was little
Don't worry I'll teach you how to say it
When I was diagnosed with Arthrogryposid
Not many doctors knew what it was
We would spend majority of the day
At Children's Memorial Hospital in Chicago
I had the coolest & badass doctor
Who did majority of my surgeries
And also was amazing at it & did a great job
He wasn't really familiar with my diagnosis
I hated going but...
The only reason I liked going
Was because I got to skip school
My mom said that sometimes
I'd be under the knife for 8-10 hours
Sometimes she would get scared & nervous
I'd get the same exact way before I went under
The one thing I absolutely hated was the gas mask
A big ole black thing covering your face
"Count from 10 to 1"

That smell was the most disgusting smell ever
There's times if I'm thinking about it
Like right this second...
My memory gets a hint of the smell & I start to gag
After I would wake up
The first thing I would want to do is eat
But I always had to wait a couple hours
My Mom would be by my bedside eating
An Coconut Mound bar
And would tease me on how good it was
After a couple of hours of sleep here & there
I'd just lay in bed watching whatever was on
Like Lamb Chop, Madeline or Mr. Rogers
One thing I loved was looking out the big window
And seeing all the other buildings lights
I always thought it was so beautiful
I'd have to stay in the boring hospital bed
For a week or two depending on what type of surgery
And how I was healing up
I always missed my siblings the most
And definitely my cozy bed
My Mom's food, definitely her food
Some days I would be so bored & sad
That my Mom would ask the nurse if we could
Take a stroll around carefully
So they would load me up in a banana cart
She'd walk slowly, and when we hit the corner
We would be flying up and down the halls
That was my favorite things to do
While cooped up in the hospital
Besides the arts and crafts or the book cart
When my doctor came in to check on me
I'd get so happy because that meant
I got to go home

I hated physical therapy
Me being me...
I'd whine about goin
And sometimes whine about doing the therapy
When I had to do at home therapy
The Occupational therapist would show
My mom how to do everything
My Mom was more strict about my therapy
So I couldn't slide out of doing it
And I definitely couldn't slack or try to

Havoc

She walked around with smiles on her face, sarcasm on her mouth, and a dark cloud above her head

Raindrops

She acted out, and pushed people away that tried to help when they saw the dark cloud

Rain Showers

The more she put the raincoat on the rain showers, the more the storm brewed inside her

Acting out more and more, and she just built a titanium shield around the storm

Lightning

She was sprinkling out tears of help, but nobody really knew actually how bad the thunderstorm was

She was ashamed, but mostly embarrassed that people would run for cover after she let the storm out

As a result, she was drowning...

WATER CYCLONE

Tainted Trust Card

"Trust me"
"Seriously, trust me"
{{Laughs}}
Seriously....
I fucking heard that more than I can count on my fingers
Trusting people has been tainted when I was a young rebel
I might sound like a complete asshole
But...
People literally have to earn my trust
"But...Ash you don't trust me?"
The answer is absolutely no
I've fed people my trust
On a vintage plater
And they left it tarnished
After they were finished
Destroying a beautiful thing
There's only been two people
Who crossed my path
That I've never had to question their trust
Besides my family those are the only two
I'd literally trust with my fucking life
See...
Before the "MONSTER" burned my trust card
I used to trust more than I do now
But...
When you are in the system
And the system "thinks" they know what you want
And think they know the best for you

They sometimes feed you to piranhas
That look like angelfish
You get lost
And feel alone
Crying
Wandering
Hoping
That someone can hear your howls
But...
Fuck...who do you trust
After...
The fucking MONSTER" annihilated your trust for good
Tell me...
Tell me...who do you fucking trust???

Visitors

I was in the 5th grade
And once again it was surgery time
This time my doctor wanted to
Straighten my hips out so that my legs were even
I have no idea what number attempts it was
But that meant...
No eating after midnight or breakfast
I was always so damn hungry
You should think I'd get used to it
Bag is packed, and back to Chicago we go
This time I was more nervous than ever
So I just looked out the window & listened to the radio
As the nurses were setting me up
I was thinking about how I wanted to run away
Already missing my siblings
Knowing I wouldn't be able to play with them for awhile
Have to eat the nasty hospital food
Well I did love the jello squares & apple juice
As the bed started to roll into the operating room
I just started to freak out
Thinking...
"What if this the last time I get to see my Mom?"
"What if I don't wake up?"
"What if they mess up?"
"I want to be with my siblings"
Even though they gave me a calming injection
I still felt on edge and wanted to flee
Then someone in the room told me to think of a song

So I thought about my Mom singing my favorite lullabies
It calmed me down
Black mask
"10, 9....out"
I woke up
My Mom was sitting next to my hospital bed
My throat was dry like the Sahara Desert
I was in extreme pain
And of course I was hungry as hell
Also extremely cold
So they gave me extra blankets
I had a neon pink cast on my whole right leg
Then I had screws & plates in my left hip
It was all bandaged up
I was bored and already sick of being cooped up
Watching some old school show on TV
That's when I heard footsteps & a knock
Thinking...
"It's time for the nurse to check my temp & vitals"
I turned my head and I couldn't believe my eyes
It was my 5th grade teachers
I was so shocked & so excited
I thought I was high off of pain meds
We talked, joked around, and laughed a lot
I had them sign my cast
My favorite teacher drew a smiley face on my big right toe
I hated my feet to be touched
But I thought it was cool that she did that
They were the only teachers ever that visited me
Maybe...I was their favorite student
{{Wink}}
So I was beyond happy about that and grateful
After a few hours they said their goodbyes
Which I didn't want them to go

They told me to recover fast so I can get back to school
I'm pretty sure I said something sarcastic
Honestly, they didn't have to come & see me
But...
They did, and I was super excited that they did
Visitor's & people like that are hard to find
And they're the best dose of medicine
Your mind, heart, and healing body needs

Pink Fluorescent Beam

Two chairs across from each other
You sit in one
I sit in the other
No touching
No talking
Everytime I think of you...
A pink aura cloud would form around me
Everytime you think of me...
A purple aura cloud would form around you
I wonder how many times...
Ours would light up at the same exact time

Dear Ink...

It took me so long...
For me to open my feelings box
Writing makes it so much easier
Because...
The ink doesn't judge you
The paper won't push you away
And…
The time doesn't pass you by
When there's tears rolling down your face
Why are people so fucking judgemental
Asking or saying something like...
Why are you crying??
You shouldn't be crying...
Boys don't cry...
No...No..no
You can't wear that, it's a boy's shirt
Girls wear pretty dresses
Why are you laughing at that??
That's not even funny
You know she's white
Why don't you date someone of your own race??
Why are you praying like that??
Take your religion somewhere else
We don't want to see that
Why are you with her??
Your lifestyle is disgusting
You're going to hell
Maybe...just maybe

That's why people shield themselves
From others & the shallow world

Eighteen

I've been a person who beats at my own drum
As if I was in a drumline battle with the world
Looking back now...
I was running & running and not looking back
From people who got close to me
Or shielding myself before anyone could hurt me
I taught myself that...
Because I thought someone who cared about me
Really didn't fucking care about me at all
Instead they mostly hurt me mentally & verbally
Mental & verbal abuse takes a toll on the mind
You start to fucking believe the serpents hiss
Then you play it over & over again in your mind
Like I said before...
I've been a person who beats at my own drum
And well...
That's what got me into trouble when I was eighteen
Waking up every fucking morning
Hating myself so deeply
That I didn't see myself in the mirror anymore
I was looking at a stranger
Like a side kick you didn't really ask for
I was jealous of my fellow classmates
Who were talking about colleges and universitie
They would ask me where I was going to school
I would say
"I don't know yet"
Or I'd just change the subject

Knowing I wasn't going to college
I was just a fucking loser
So...
I was in a situation that got me kicked out of my house
Swimming in an ocean of nowhere
I gave up on everything
Not caring what happened to me
I was literally fucking drowning
Then a family that knew our family took me in
I didn't know what to think or how to feel at the time
They took me in like their own
But I was still...
Drowning but in a new environment
I would cry silently into my pillow
So no one could hear me or ask questions
I was missing my siblings
Honestly that was my fault for my ignorant actions
Minutes turned to hours
Hours turned into days
Days turned into weeks
Weeks turned into months
I didn't have any friends anymore
Because high school was over
I couldn't see my siblings
So I thought about them every fucking day
Hoping & wishing that they were doing well
I remember...
One day I was missing my siblings so fucking bad
I was laying in bed as tears rolled down my face
Then I heard music playing in the next room
Just laying there I kept listening
Then I got up and went to the room
A girl with blonde hair & blue eyes
With a genuine bubbly personality

Was just jumping on her bed
And singing along to the song
I heard the song before
And it reminded me of home
But I didn't remember who sang ot
"Who sings that?"
"She Daisy"
She responded as she kept jumping
I entered the room to keep listening
Then I just started dancing too
That moment made me so happy
Happiest that I've felt in the longest time
We listened to more music
She didn't make me want to run
I honestly believed...
She was going to be my best friend down the road
I trusted her right off bat
And honestly that never happens
I never had to question her loyalty
After awhile we did a lot of things together
Whenever I was being an asshole or in a funk
She'd let me figure it out
And then everything was all good
After I calmed down
Years and years went by
And we still remained friends
She surely was my best friend
She accepted me for me and nothing less
She never judged me because I was different
She treated me like a "normal" person
Never excluded me but knew my limit
Years down the line...
Picked my pen back up
And let the ink bleed

She was the first person to read my words
I thought she was going say it was bad
But honestly it was the opposite
Now it's 2020...
And our friendship is still strong
Eighteen years strong like titanium
She still encourages me to keep writing
And I love sharing my words with her
Honestly...
I'm fucking lucky that she's my best friend
I WOULDN'T trade it for anything in this world

Rookie

I was never part of a soccer or chess team
Honestly...
I always wanted to be part of something
I wanted to belong
Wanted that varsity jacket
That 1st place trophy
I realized...
I was looking into the wrong sport
The wrong team
When...
I picked up my pen & notebook
And put dedication & passion into it
Day in and day out
I am a...
WRITER
I am on a Writer's League
I swear I'll get that trophy
A round of applause, please
It will be...
A published book
That I poured my heart & dedication into

Suffocation

I'll never forget my first panic attack
It was two weeks after the death of my older brother
It definitely was unexpected
We were all extremely shocked and sad
I was sad & also worried about my Mom's well being as well
Because they were inseparable
And now she felt alone
Even though she had us by her side
Anyways...
My mom was cooking dinner
And my sister was in the kitchen
I was watching TV starting to feel weird
My heart started racing extremely fast like a stopwatch
But 4x the speed
I stood up quickly
Walked into the kitchen
Fuck...
Their voices are so damn loud
The light is extremely bright
Closing my eyes for a few seconds
Then I opened them
Oh fuck...
I can't breathe
Starting to gag
Trying to catch my breath
"Mom there's something wrong"
"What?"
"I don't know...I can't breathe"

Trying to catch my breath
Over & over again
My hands started feeling numb
Thinking...
Oh fuck, I'm dying
I'm having a heart attack
No...maybe a stroke
Hands numb & sweaty
My sister comes in the kitchen
She hands me a glass of water
Trying to swallow the water
And trying to breath is impossible
She told me to sit down on the couch
I couldn't move
Why couldn't I move
"Mom, please help me"
"Ash, what do you want me to do"
"I don't know...I'm scared"
"Can you sit down"
Now I'm halfway in the kitchen doorway
Everything around me was heightened
My mouth was so dry
Like a mouth full of cotton
Still trying to catch my breath
My sister looking at me
"Ash please sit down, you need to sit"
I sat on the arm of the couch
My heart beating rapidly
Like it wants to pop out of my chest
Now my legs feel weak & numb
"Mom..."
My mom picks up her phone
And calls 911
As she's on the phone

She kept asking me questions
I couldn't really remember the answers to them
I heard my Mom say
"She's having trouble breathing, and she's a little pale"
My sister was gathering my meds & stuff
As the ambulance came
They checked my vitals
Then the guy was saying he remembered me
When they came to get my brother a few weeks ago
He was explaining to me that I was having a panic attack
I asked him if he was sure
"Yes, you have all the signs"
By now I was feeling better
He asked me if they needed to take me in
I looked at my Mom
"No, we'll keep an eye on her"
They checked my vitals again
The rest of the evening my Mom kept checking on me
"Ash, your color came back"
That night I couldn't sleep because I was too scared to

Levels

My mind is kind of...
Like the game of Tetris
All the thoughts are coming down fast
In beautiful fluorescent colors
Of purple, pink, dark teal, and white
Each word that drops down
I pick carefully as I ink it out
On the pages of my notebook
It will stay permanently inked
In a beautiful complete sentence
I won't be completely satisfied
Until I finish...
My beautiful colorful masterpiece of poetry & stories
Then I'll think to myself
"Ash...it's time to..."
BOOM...
Level up

Hummingbird Friendship Forever

(Dedicated To My Best Friend)

She was a wild one
They tried to tame her
The more they wanted to put her in a cage
The more she rebelled more and more
All her wildness wanted...
Was for them to understand the firestorm she fought everyday
But...
Instead they judged her and called her trouble
So the wild grew stronger
Until...
One person entered her wild
Ran along with her without judgement
With amazing little adventures
Her wild world now has phoenixes & hummingbirds
Flying above all the ashes and sunsets
Because...
Of that one soul that understood
HER WILD

Heartbreak & Temporary Love

I'm putting my loving heart back on the shelf
Were people keep old dusty boxes
My mind & soul is slowly not believing in true love
I've done it...
Cupid's way
Long Distance's way
And even around the corner's way
Every single time my heartstrings gets used & fucked with
The last woman done me & my heart in good
I thought she was perfect
But all she wanted to do was to test my mustang
And get her fix on temporary happiness
I'm thinking right now...
That there's nobody out there for me anymore
Sick & tired of people using my loving heart for a doormat
Because...
They aren't happy in theirs
Or they're "taking" a break
Wanting that temporary love & the temporary happiness
I let my stupid feelings over power my decisions & actions
When I like someone I like them way too fucking hard
Or they don't really like me
But still suck up my flirtatious coins
Like I'm an vintage arcade game
I'm asking myself on the daily
"What does falling in love really truly feel like?"
Because...
What I'm feeling doesn't feel like anything

But...
Heartbreak

Dreams

When I was younger...
I wanted to be so many things when I grew up
I wanted to be a model
But...
I never seen someone that looked like me
So I let that dream sail away
Then…
I wanted to be an athlete
Either a soccer or basketball player
But...
I knew I couldn't play soccer
Because my legs wouldn't be fast enough
Then I was like…
Well basketball isn't all that hard
Because I would play background basketball with my siblings all the time
So...
I begged my Mom to let me play in intramurals basketball
We had to get my doctor's approval because I kept begging
He told me to give it a try
So I played the game, and yes I loved it
The only two things though…
One, I didn't have the magic fade away
Nor did I have the physical endurance
So again, I let that dream sail away
Couple years went by
Then one time of many groundings
I was extremely bored

So...
I started writing in an old green notebook
I just let the pen flow along the blank lines
Honestly, it felt so fucking natural
Like it was always in my soul
As if the ink has always been in my veins
I kept writing in the notebook
Until it was full of ink
Then someone had to piss on my dream
Saying...
"You aren't smart enough to be a writer"
"You have to be a great reader"
I took that notebook and threw it away
That was the night I laid awake for a few hours
Then I cried myself to sleep
That morning I felt so low
I stopped dreaming
And whenever someone asked what I wanted to be
I just shrugged and said "I don't know"
See...
I always thought about writing
If I sat in the car
I'd watch people walk by
Then make up stories about them
I'd always watch my siblings
And thought of them as different characters
Then...
One day I wrote a fanfic and showed it to my best friend
She said it was really good
I felt a mixture of shock and honored all at once
I let that marinate in my mind
My dream of being a writer
Started to come forward a little bit
Years passed by

And I started to realize
I was a very lost soul
Not knowing who I really was anymore
I was fading away even though
I still could see my reflection in the mirror
Myself couldn't recognize myself
In 2018 I picked my pen back up
It was the only thing that helped me
Keep some of my fucked up mind quite
I sent my writings to my best friend
Once again she liked them
So...
This I used that as a motivation to keep writing
I kept letting the ink bleed
Bleed
Bleed
Bleed
Then I found a community that I actually fit in with
I can say that I've made a handful
Of genuine souls that I'm honored to call my friends
Like I said...
It felt fucking natural
Like it was always in my soul
As if the ink has always been in my veins
Let me rephrase that...
It's fucking natural
It's always been in my soul
The ink has always flowed through my veins

Changeless

Looking in the mirror has always been hard for me
Accepting who I was definitely a huge struggle
Me accepting that I was gay
It was like...
Walking with bricks on my shoulders
And bombs strapped to my chest
I wanted this heavyweight thing
Off of me every single day
I didn't know what was happening to me
Thinking...
Fuck, she's so beautiful...why do I want to kiss her?!
Fuck...why do I get butterflies when she walks by?
Damn...she has gorgeous eyes
Honestly...
I couldn't tell anyone what was brewing
Inside of my emotions & mind
I fault it like an MMA fighter
Some nights I would fucking cry
Intomy pillow until I fell asleep
Why...
Why couldn't I just scream it out
And just be happy like everyone else
Six grade...
Six grade was the hardest for me
Because that's when I got strong feelings for a classmate
She was so beautiful, smart, funny & kind
Could I tell her that?
No...No...No

I was fucking dying inside
Like someone was holding my fucking life hostage
In my early 20's...
I finally got the guts to tell one of my best friends
I got on the computer and wrote an email
After I finished it I was thinking…
Just press send
No...wait...wait...okay...press it
That same day my heart was racing
Like a fucking stallion race horse
I checked my email
And I got a message back
It was a very accepting message
I felt so many bricks fall off of my shoulders
Next...
I decided to tell my other best friend
She's known me ever since I was like 6 years old
I was super nervous to tell her
But it easier to let it out this time
She was very, very accepting
Another ton of bricks fell off of my shoulders
But..
I still have this big bomb
That I needed to dislodge from my chest
The hardest person to tell was my Mom
I wanted to do it face to face
Just her and I alone
But....
That never fucking happened
It was more like a yelling match
She wasn't listening, and didn't want to listen
Honestly...
I was glad it got out
But not the way that I had planned

I still felt the bomb in my chest
And I knew it wasn't ever going to dislodge
Fuck...
I can't change who I am
And honestly I wouldn't want to
It took me so fucking long to accept who I am
I slowly started loving myself
Instead of waking up every morning hating myself
Then picking myself apart
Hiding myself behind a mask
I'm...
Proud of who I am
And...
I'll never fucking change

My Security Blanket

Another long ride to the hospital
Chicago bound, majority of the day
Mom's perfume in the air
Check in...Paperwork...Waiting room
Mom reading a magazine
Little girl with beads in her hair
AFOs on her string bean legs
Looking at the fish in the big tank
Name called...
Nerves kicking in
Weigh in & measure height recorded
Exam room, with white walls & bright lights
Mom helping put on the oversized gown on
Thin white paper crinkles on the exam bed
Little girls legs dangling over the edge
Nervous...
How much longer
Patiently waiting for the doctor
Holding in her hand was a little figurine
A Hello Kitty with a red bow & blue dress
This was her...
SECURITY BLANKET

The World Needs A Little More Joy In It

(Dedicated To My Best Friend)

I'm a person who doesn't open up easily like a clam shell
I honestly don't offer my trust on a silver platter
You have to earn it like a trophy
I believe you'll cherish it more & forever
I surely didn't expect to have an amazing friend like you
Honestly...
You never limited me because of my disability
You knew how much I could handle
But, still was close enough to help me if I struggled
You treated me like a "normal" person
I never had to question your trust
Or loyalty like I do with everyone else
I love how you didn't frown upon my passion for writing
You've encouraged me to keep going
That's what fuels me up every time
My ink bleeds on the paper
You understand how my quirky mind
I wish you knew how important you
And our friendship is to me
I surely honor it like it's the rarest gold
That I have ever found in my life
So...
Thank you for being my best friend
And seeing me for me
Honestly...
There needs to be more people like you in this world

Iconic Dance

She didn't care if you
Were Black or White
She loved the iconic dance
The moon walk
Damn...
She was a Smooth Criminal
On the dance floor
Her name wasn't Billie Jean
But...
She could be my lover

Roots Of My Soul

Flipping through these pages of my notebook
Honestly...
I can't believe I've written
All of these masterpieces
That all started as a seed
As I bled ink droplets of me
From the ink of my pen
Acted like it was water
And gave them life
It grew into a strong Cherry Blossom Tree
I inked pieces of my soul
Inside it's majestic roots

Super Love

Don't be mad when you see that her bags are gone
She's going Rogue
You played too much with her heart
Like Gambit
And froze out her heart
Like Iceman
She can't take the cold anymore
She needs someone to warm her soul & heart
Like Pyro

Oxygen Mask

Whoever captures my heart…
Needs to have strong strapping lungs
And has to have a strong air flow
Because...
I'll always love seeing her smile
I'll always love seeing her laugh
I'll always love hearing her giggles
And...
Once we say "I do"
I'll always try my very fucking best
To keep that gorgeous smile on her face
And keep her laughing that contagious laugh
Even on our darkest days
Til my very last breath

My Dream & Passion

Yes, one day I want to see a book I've written
On shelves of bookstores or anywhere
Like under my "future" son's pillow
We're he sneaks and reads it
Late at night with a flashlight
On a teenagers night stand
Or in the back pocket of a rebellion boy
Who reads my pages to his boyfriend
Either way I want my name on something
So the people who loved me
Or encouraged me to keep my dream alive
Have little pieces of me when I leave this world

California Sunsets

I love a lot of things in nature wise...
I love anything body of water
The sound of the waves hitting the rocks
Or...
When the waves hit the shoreline
It's so beautiful when the the water is still as scared mino
And the sun reflection paints the trees & sky
Over the beautiful glass of water
I love the sound of waterfalls
Falling into a big bay of water
Or when you jump off the ledge
Into the pool of gorgeous water
But...
I absolutely love sunsets
And for some reason…
The sun that sets in the west seems more majestic
More vibrantly gorgeous
You just look up...
And it just looks like an artist has painted the sky
I feel so alive whenever I look at it
In a warm gorgeous atmosphere
With the crickets singing
And the lighting bugs blinking
I swear...
The sunsets in the west are the most gorgeous scenery
I've laid my brown eyes on

Gladiator Wings

(Dedicated to my little brother)

Lake waves singing
Paddle boats rides under the hot beaming sun
Fishing Pole
Mastering to get the hook in the carpet
On his birthday every single time
Flea Market Adventures
King Of the Raft
Four Square Tournaments
Collecting unique rocks
Pog Tournaments
Makes the sloppiest PB&J sandwiches
Sand castles
Watching Gladiator & Ed, Edd, & Eddy on weekends
Bird Whisperer
A boy with Sandy blonde hair
Summer tan from the summer sun rays
With Superman ice cream all over his lips
Teaching his older sister how to skip rocks
Taken too soon from his family
Now in paradise…
With the most majestic wings you ever did see

Within My Words

Perhaps one day she'll find my notebooks
Full of poetry and short stories
She'll fall in love with them
As how I fell head over sneakers in love with her
She'll say...
"These are beautiful"
I'll say...
"Not as beautiful as you my love"
She'll smile that smile that melts my heart
Like on a humid summer day
I'll kiss those silk soft lips
As if it was our very first kiss
Then I'll say...
"My love, you are my poetry"

Societies Shackles

Society is a sick bitch with a horrible tricks up her sleeve

They fucking paint a beautiful facade of how people should...

Live

Love

See...

If you look at the first fine coat of paint, you'll see the fucking flaws that were actually there

Who the fuck wrote these fucked up visions of how someone should live their one and only life

Because....

I'd like to thank you for how fucking shallow you look every single damn day

Listen...

I never understood why people had the donkey Kong balls to dictate how I should live. Or how I should think. Tell me what I need or fucking want.

Always feeling like I was trapped in a dark cage, with chains on my feet, and even if I tried to speak, nothing would come out.

You broke me
You fucking broke me

I broke into a fucking jigsaw puzzle, where all the pieces are floating above my head, and I can't fucking reach any pieces of me.

You see…

I was in a loving home, where a Mom loved me, where my siblings loved me, where I had a bed, clothes on my back, and my favorite toys to play with, and food in my belly.

But apparently...

Society had to make a decision...or let's say fuck with my mind & heart.
Meaning...a white Mother raising and loving a black child apparently isn't good enough in society's eyes. That only a black Mother can raise and love a black child better than a white Mother can.

So...

Let's take her out of an environment that was perfect for her, and put her into an environment that you think a black child should need...a black mother.

Well...

Society, you fucked up on that one. The new environment was cold, lonely, and unlovable.

The color of your skin doesn't define how well you can take care of a child. Or how to love a child. It's that big red muscle that pumps in your chest.

I struggled through my whole life trying to accept & love myself. Some days were better than others. I knew I was different, but I didn't understand why. I sometimes thought maybe I did something wrong, or something...just didn't know what.

I could see that I was different, especially whenever I went into public. People would stare, whisper into another person's ear, sometimes kids who didn't understand would stare, or point at me. I always pretended it never bothered me, but deep down it tore me apart.

So...

I've always made sure I had something to fucking prove, I had to prove fucking society that she was fucking wrong about me.

I could do that, but in my own way
I adapted to a world that wasn't built for me
Oh... society you know that white woman who you thought wasn't suitable to care for me...

Well...

She's the one who taught me how to adapt to this fucked up world.

{{CLAPS}}

Besides having a disability, I also was struggling with something else. Something I didn't know how to tell anybody, because I thought I was the only one like this. I definitely struggled with this.

"Oh she's so cute!"
"Why do I get butterflies whenever she's near me?"
"Oh I'd love to kiss her!"

I would have posters up of guys, as a decoy, but I'd always look at the girls in the magazines. I never told anyone about this. I would sometimes cry at night in my pillow, hoping my sister's didn't hear me because I felt so alone. I wanted answers.

Then...

I was in public once, and there were two guys in the gap store. Minding their own business, and I heard...

"What a bunch of fags"
"You're going to burn in hell"

I looked at the two guys, one guy had his arm around the other guys neck. I wasn't thinking anything of it, until it clicked. I felt my whole heart shatter for those guys who were trying to enjoy their shopping day.
I honestly started hating society like it was a 9-5 job...
I had to fight my thoughts about myself
I started to hate myself more & more

My feet were shackled to cement, as my soul was in jigsaw puzzle pieces.

After awhile...

I paused...and stopped worrying or thinking what society was whispering to me. So I slowly started to break free, and said....

"Fuck you society, fuck you"

Respect

I was the little girl, with the witty attitude, who wore beads and barretts in my hair, wore pink dresses and girly clothes.

I was also that awkward teenage girl who pretended to like boys to make others happy, especially my family. I was drowning and exhausted pretending to be someone I wasn't. I hated myself so damn much.

I'm not that little girl or that teenager anymore...

I'm a woman with the same witty attitude, who feels more ALIVE when my hair is short. When I wear hoodies and jeans, or when I wear snapbacks and bandanas. I love when a beautiful woman compliments my smile. I don't feel like I'm drowning anymore because I'm not pretending anymore.

You don't need to like how I live or who I love, but it would be great if you could just **RESPECT** me. I never once asked you to pretend or hide your true self.

Because...

I'll always be that little girl with a witty attitude in your eyes. I'll always need you in my corner, when no one else is.

Ignite

You ignited my heart
Now my soul is on fire

Scars

Your visible scars are like tattoos
Behind each one is a story
When you look at them it'll remind you of a struggle

But..

They motivated you to move forward
Gives you strength to stay strong
Added courage even when you wanted to give up

Mine gave me...

Strength
&
Determination

So wear yours loud and proud

Demon Whispers

She lays in her bed
In the darkness
As the sound of her show echoes off the walls
As she tries to sleep
But...
Yet again the demons whispers
Floods her mind with poison
She closes her eyes tightly
Trying to think over the demons whispering
"STOP...."
"SHUT UP...."
Hours of the night tossing & turning
Eyes heavy as bricks
Well, hello...
INSOMNIAC

Roots Of A Willow Tree

You were the beautiful Willow tree
And I was the dirt that caressed
Your warm loving roots
All I wanted was for you to be loved
All season round
Underneath the moon's reflection
And grow to your fullest peak
On a hot summer days

Megaphone

I'm NOT doing this to be famous
Nor for the likes
I'm doing this to be heard
Have my words marinate in your minds
To those…
Who like to judge the misunderstood souls
To help that...
Boy sitting in the dark trying to breathe
Because he's struggling with depression & anxiety
To help that...
Girl who cries at night because she's made fun
Because she's into other girls
To help that…
Little quirky girl that has a disability
Who walks with a walker with attitude
Listen up...
Please, stop dictating what someone can & can't do
Because you don't know what someone is capable of doing
And trust me…
If you tell them they can't do something
They'll keep doing it til they prove you wrong

My Mom's Perfume

She always snuck into her mother's bathroom, when she was younger

Opened up the perfume, and sprayed a little on her shirt.

She felt at ease whenever she smelled the perfume

Especially when...

She would wake up from her surgeries

Because it felt like her Mother's arms were around her, and it always felt like...

HOME
&
SAFE

Dripn' Temptations

She smelled summertime breeze and coffee
Her lips were so damn sexy
Damn...
Her kisses were so smoking hot
Like the Sahara Desert
My mouth was a thirst trap
Like the Niagara Falls

Paper Treasures

I think I was 9 or 10
When I got my first love letter
Receiving it from my summer love
Who had to leave camp early
I remember when I got it
I opened it carefully, unfolded it slowly
Read every line
As if it was some kind of hidden code
I remember the last line
"I love you, love your Alex"
That was my favorite line
Because he was the first person
Who said those loving words to me
It was my first & only love letter I've received
I folded it up exactly how he did
Then carefully put it back into the envelope
Carrying it around like a little treasure
I cherished it with all my heart
Maybe...
That's why I like writing them & giving the
Because whenever she misses me...
She can just pull it out & read it
As it sends warm love to her heart

Gorgeous Spell

Don't look into her eyes
Especially on a full moon
It's her gorgeous weapon in disguise
That's how she compelled me into her love spell

Finer Things

She's finer than vintage wine
So pour me up baby
Because...
I'm about to get drunk off of your love

Prince With Wings

(Dedicated to my little brother)

He had blue eyes like the ocean
Blonde hair like the summer sands
A smile like a prince
Fierce fighter like a gladiator

Escaping In My Ink

I write to escape the real world
The world has beautiful majestic colors
But....
Society & certain people
Drain the fucking color right out of it
They fucking drip black & white
Madness paint over something beautiful
I look up to the cotton candy clouds
And...
It's raining boiling raindrops
Instead...
Of sweet sparkling raindrops
I write to escape the real world
These characters I build DNA for
Are a little dash of Ash in them
If I sat with each one of them
Each one of them would understand me
They wouldn't push me away
Or think I'm truly fucked up
Because...
They're sailing in the same boat as I am
They're all flawed with a big heart
But mostly misunderstood
And...
That's how I look at myself
Or...
Maybe my reflection is...
Just fucking lying to me

Wild Vivacity

Wanting her to wear her halo like a princess
So she obeyed them with a fake smile
Until she saw her...
Swaying her beautiful hips
With a glass of vodka in one hand
And singing along to the filthy lyrics
That's when...
She traded her halo in for her freedom

Sexy & Sleek

She got that drip in her walk
Every time she sways her hips
My eyes are fucking hypnotized
My brown irises has a orgasmic pulse
She's a fucking independent queen
The only time she needs assistance
Is when she wants me to pipe her down
With my filthy savage tongue
She loves it when I swim deep
Between her thick thighs
She bad like Anne Hathaway
Especially when she wears Prada
Got damn...
She makes me wanna fucking sin like Lucifer

Static Nightmare

I feel like I'm living in a repeat nightmare
That's playing on an old classic television
Where's the remote
Remote...Remote...where is it
Oh found it...
Click
Click
Click
What the fuck
Checks the batteries
No batteries
Fuck...
I'll just switch it manually
Channel 3
Static
Channel 7
Static
Channel 16
Static
What the fucking hell
Stands up
Walks over to the television
Smacks the side of the television
{{Smack}}
{{Smack}}
Looks into the static screen
I see my reflection
The reflection is mimicking me

Wait...
What...
{{Zap}}
Now I'm inside the television
Dark
Cold
Empty
Screams...
"Hello"
"Anybody out there?
{{Tapping}}
I start to punch the thick glass
My knuckles start to get bloody and bruised
I scream as loud as I could
Punching the thick glass on last time
I slide down into a slump
And tears...
Just come seeping out down my tired sad face

Abstract

She's the ocean waves crashing against my ribs
Taking my breath away like a beautiful sunset
She's the color of my universe
She's a vibrant abstract masterpiece
That...
Colors my soul with her love

Acoustic Love Strings

Her perfume lingers on my shirt
As she pushed her body against mine
She imprints her lips onto my bare neck
Like a beautiful vintage tattoo
Her love plays off my ribcage
Like lyrics off of a beautiful acoustic guitar
My heart beats ocean waves
As her love crashes into my soul

Destination

Flying above the west coast
Is such a beautiful view
Lights flickering like bright lite
And looking like a giants blueprint
Landing at my favorite destination
For the second time in my life
Waiting to step foot on warm grounds
A guy with a surfers vibe
Wished me a chill visit
Then he hit me a happiest mellow smile
I was tired as hell
But, the Cali air hit my cheeks
I felt a different kind of happiness
Palm trees looking tall & majestic
I'm at my favorite destination
Hello, California

Savage Beast Mode

Look at me, please
Hey...
Hey, chin up
Don't cover those scars
Let them shine like the fierce wolf that you are
They didn't have to fight on that dark battlefield
That you had to claw your way out and overcome
Hey
Hey, chin up
Look at me, please
Let me see that…
Savage Alpha Omega that you are
Inhale
Exhale
DEEP GROWL
Now...
Unleash the beast

Gunslinger Romance

I was her Clyde
And she was my Bonnie
She stole my heart
Like city slickers on the run
Her halo was definitely dirty
Shit...
Her badass status was on fire
She always made me wanna sin
Like Lucifer on a hot summers night
Fuck...
That girl was bad to the fucking max

Calm Eyes

When you look into my eyes
I want you to find the love you deserve
Feel safe whenever you step foot in the front door
As I hug you tightly in my arms
I want you to instantly feel calm
And feel at home
Because...
My love, my forever
That's what I want to feel
Every single time I lay my eyes on you

Strawberry Margaritas

Our majestic fort made of palm tree leafs
Exotic flowers as you walk in
Come on my love
Let's sip on some delicious strawberry margaritas
As we cuddle each other
And give unlimited Eskimo kisses & forehead kisses
We'll swim as the the sun glistens
On our beautiful summer skin
I'll sneak in little kisses
As mother nature paints
The sky full of beautiful colors
When the night falls black
We'll build a cozy huge fire
Sit with blankets around us
As I read my poetry
And you play your guitar
When your eyes get heavy
I'll lay with you
As we softly kiss
Until we both drift into dreamland

Windy City Beauty

Boarding the plane tired and hungry
That's when she spoke a beautiful harmony
Medium dark brown hair
Brown eyes of a goddess
Secretary looking glasses
That fit perfectly on her cabbage patch cheeks
Her smile made me smile
Thinking...
Damn she's beautiful
Strike up a conversation
Ask for her number
Deeper thinking...
No she's being nice because it's her job
No she wouldn't be into me
Especially someone like me
Anyways...
I was just memorized by her beauty
Her kindness in her soul & smile
Every time she walked up & down the aisle
Our eyes would lock in on each other
She would smile
I'd smile back
Plane is landing....
Everyone is leaving
She walks towards me
Strikes up a conversation
Telling me she's only been working this job for three years
She told me she never been to L.A

And that she's always wanted to see The Walk Of Fame
I told her she needed to go sometime
Because I loved it two years ago when I first went
She said...
"This sounds lame, I've always wanted to see Marilyn Monroe star"
I said...
"It's not lame at all"
She smiled at me
It was my time to leave
She said...
"Have a nice flight home"
I smiled and said...
"Thank you, and I hope you get to go to L.A"
She said...
"I hope so, and it would be fate if we ran into each other again"
I said..
"That would be awesome"
Then I just smiled
She sketched beautiful lyrics into my soul
And...
If fate has it for us to meet again
Then I'd be on humbled and honored

Chariote Heart Stone

I close my eyes
And all I can see
You and your beautiful smile
If...
If you were mine to love
When I opened my eyes
I'd tell you every day
How lucky I am to have you in my presence
How damn lucky to love you
How lucky to look into your gorgeous eyes
How damn lucky that I get to kiss those luscious lips
How lucky to hold you in my once lonely arms
Every night that the moon and stars ignite the sky
I would...
Tell you how gorgeous you are
Even when you think you look terrible
Wipe your tears as they fell from your eyes
Because you were feeling defeated on a bad day
I'd embrace you with my loving arms until you fell asleep
And fight any demons that try to darken your mind
Give you all the extra kisses & cuddles that you crave
I'll try to grant your wishes
Even though you think there silly
I'd make love to you every time
I would want you to feel every bit of my love
As you moan in pleasure
Because...
In my eyes you are 1 in a million

The most gorgeous charoite stone that I ever found in the rough
And...
I'd be the happiest soul if you called me
YOURS

Cherry Crepes

Trace my finger along her lower lip
Soft like the silk sheets
Draping over our naked curves
Passionate kisses delicate as a flower
Biting your lower lip softly
As if it's a plump cherry
That I tease you slowly with
As I dangle it over your mouth
So damn delicious...
As a cherry filled crepe
Topped off with creamy whipped cream

The Moonlight Ocean

Opening lines is the hardest part
So...
I wouldn't know what to say
If she was in my space
I'd admire her like the beautiful sunset
Her eyes have waves
From the ocean white caps
My heart is swaying
Like the palm trees in the West Coast
She rocks my boat
Making me seasick
Because...
Her beauty is so damn captivating
I want to anchor my heart at her dock
And stay forever under her moonlight & stars

Curve Ball

My thoughts are being selfish
Thinking...
Why you?
Why this way?
What if?
I know I can't turn back time
Because...
If I could I'd bring you back
I'd give you a healthy body
But the same personality
Life throws you curveballs
And....
Sometimes you can't catch them until it's too late

Love Marks

I want to see the want of temptations in your eyes
As I softly kiss up & down your spine
With my tender full lips
Let me sketch my love mark
On your sweet luscious neck
You gripping the silk lavender sheets
Arching your back like a contemporary dancer
As I tease & kiss your inner thighs
Let me inhale your ecstasy
As you exhale your falsetto moans

Temptation Tales

I want to get lost in your adventurous eyes
Like how I get lost in my ink tales
Every time we kiss
I want to taste your lips
As if they were sweet fruit punch
Intertwine your legs around my waist
As we foreplay to deep temptations
I want you to get lost in an orgasmic bliss

The One & Only

If the day comes where she floats into my life
I know my heart will be pumping hummingbirds
And my rib cage will be blooming tiger lilies
I'll love her unconditionally beyond our galaxy
With all my being...
I'll do my very fucking best to keep her happy
We'll never ever go to bed mad at each other
Each & every time we leave the house or anything
It'll be my obligation to tell her
"I LOVE YOU"
I'll be so lucky to introduce her to my two best friends
In my heart I'll know they'll love her
Because they'll see...
The happiness beaming from my soul
And to the ones...
Who missed out on knowing her
Well let's just say...
I'm sorry for your ignorance
Because you'll be missing out on a loving soul
Who loves me unconditionally
And won't ever try to change me
But she'll want me...
To succeed in and everything I do
And I'll know..
When it's time to say
"I DO"
I'll be bursting with extreme happiness
Of our favorite colors of confetti

When we finally kiss...
Our moment will freeze frame
And all you'll hear is…
Both of our hearts beat as one

Her Wild World

She was a wild one
They tried to to tame her
The more they wanted to put her in a cage
She rebelled more & more
All her wild wanted
Was for them to understand
The firestorm she always had to fight everyday
But...
Instead they judged her and called her trouble
So the wild grew stronger
Until...
One person entered her wild world
Ran along with her without judgement
With amazing little adventures they had
Her wild world now has, always will have
Phoenix & Hummingbirds
Flying above all the ashes and sunsets
Because...
Of that one soul that understood
HER WILD

Bloody Tongue

You either...
Love me
Or you either...
Hate me
I don't go around trying
To make people like me anymore
If you hate me for being me
Or sticking up for myself
Then...
Fucking hate me
Because at the end of the day
You're the one who's actually
Hating yourself on a deeper level
That's why you have two devils
Whispering hate in your ears
And you blurt out the toxic fire
That's brewing inside you
But...
Don't understand estimate me
Because, even if I don't say a word
I'm biting my fucking tongue
Trying not to say a fucking word
Shhhh....
The inner wolf in me is ready to be let loose
And...
Once that wolf is out of its cage
I'm not going to be able to control it for long
Once it tastes the blood on it's tongue

The hot breath of words
Will fucking chase you down
READY
SET
RUN
The fucking wolf is out
Once it's done defending itself
It'll howl at the fucking full moon
On a full stomach of...
VICTORY

Mighty Mouse

(Dedicated To My Little Sister)

I'm not giving up on you
Because...
You would never give up on me
I know your recovery road
Is a long ahead of you
And...
I'll try my fucking best to be your cheerleader
I know what it feels like to struggle
I know how it feels like to give up
I know how it feels like to get frustrated
What you need to remember
Is that you're a fucking fighter
You've been through hell & back
I'm fucking proud of how far you've fought
Now...
I know my strength isn't like it used to be
But, I've got some tips & tricks up my sleeve
I know you'll get tired
That's when…
You can take a break
I know you'll get frustrated
That's when...
You can take a break
I know you'll want to give up
Guess what...
We aren't about that
You'll take a break and try again

We'll keep trying & trying
So...
Listen up Mighty Mouse
It's fucking game time

Rain Chronicles

I've always loved the sound of the rain
It sounds like chimney sweepers dancing
On a vintage tin roof
A massage therapist on the go
When you get hit by the downpour
Angel tears as they drip on the streets
That are surrounded by caution tape
Because…
They couldn't save the person they were protecting
Contemporary dancers dancing on the ocean
Like I said...
I've always loved the sound of the rain
It drops tiny heart droplets
Throughout my anatomy

Wild Sneakers

You were wild crazy
But...
The funny kinda wild crazy
Maybe....
That's why I fell head over sneakers
In love with you

Sweet Stings

The sight is so sweet
That it stings the soul
But...
Don't taint the beauty
Because it might erupt the queen

Morse Code

It's been 14 years since
You took your last breathes in this world
But...
It still feels like it was yesterday
I'm not going to lie or sugar coat this
It fucking sucks that you aren't here
I always think about you
I always wonder...
What would you look like today
What profession you would've been
Would we still be close & be partners in crime
Would you have tons of kids
Who are running wild looking like you
Would you let me be that crazy Aunt
Telling your kids stories about you
I know they would bust a lung laughing
I'm still friends with my best friend
You were right…
That she was gonna become my best friend
Since I've been writing again
I've met some really amazing talented friends
I was just talking to one about you
Showing her a picture of you too
She said you were handsome
I smiled because she was totally correct
Looking up to the dark sky full of stars
Is the only way I can talk to you now
Sometimes I wish…

You would give me a morse code with the stars
Telling me that you are fine
I still cry sometimes when I miss you
Sometimes I even write about our silly memories
Fuck..
I wouldn't change them for anything
In this dark, black & white world
Sorry not sorry that this is long
I just miss the fuck out of you
My little gladiator with wings

Flashlight

I hate when people say
"You can't always be this happy"
First...
I would like for you to walk a mile in my sneakers
Second...
I'm not going to lie
I've always been an angry soul
I've tore myself apart every fucking day
Inside my fucked up mind
I was dancing with the demons
Because they knew me more than most
I was taught to survive & adapt to a world
That wasn't built for me
I have an independent lone wolf badge
When people got close to me
I'd push them away before they could hurt me
People make promises that they can not keep
So...
Trust is a big thing for me
You have to earn it
And if you crinkle it
Then it's crinkled forever
No way trying to fix what we once had
Loyalty is like gold to me
Steal it from me
And I'll get Ursula after you
What ever respect you dish out
Is the same respect I'll give to you

Listen...
I hated myself for the longest time
I wandered around this world like a ghost
Trying to figure out who I was
Trying to figure out what my fucking purpose was
I was drowning real deep
When I lost my little brother in 2005
It was the hardest thing I had to deal with
I didn't understand why he had to go so soon
He didn't get to do a lot of things
And here I am
Angry
Angry
Angry
I started writing again
But then I put my pen down like a coward
Because I didn't think I was good
Still searching for who I was
Thinking...
What was my purpose
Then I just told myself I was nothing
That I was just a fucking loser
February 18th, 2018...
Was another dark & hardest day for our family
Especially for my Mom
Who I think is the strongest soul ever
I asked for prayers
We even prayed in the hospital room
I even fucking prayed so hard
Then the doctors said
"1%"
I re-said that in my mind
Over & over again
So the strongest woman that I known

Had to make the hardest decision of her life
That day we all said goodbye to my older brother
Few weeks after...
Was when I almost lost my Mom
That's when my mind started to brew havoc
I was fucking scared
I was fucking lost
I felt so fucking alone
I started to get angry
I picked up phone my on the way home from the hospital
I just started typing what was on my mind
After I finished what I wrote
I literally started crying
And a brick fell off my chest
BOOM
That's also when Miss Depression & Miss Anxiety
Knocked at my dark, dark door
Everyday I would have an attack
I was so tired
I was so lost
I couldn't take it anymore
I would cry
Then get angry
Then cry
REPEAT
One night I was so deep in my head
I was thinking about the unthinkable
That's when I knew I needed fucking help
I told the doctor what was going on
So she gave me these "delicious" happy pills
People can call me weak
And guess what...
I don't give a fuck
I started to feel more upbeat

Laying in my bed I started crying
Not because I was sad
But because I was starting to feel like me
I kept a pen & notebook by my side
One poem
Two poems
Turned into many poems and stories
This has been the longest that my ink has bled
The longest I've kept something going
My best friend told me to keep writing
So I've listened to her advice
That's when I started to feel more alive
I've met so many talented people
In the writing community
They also helped me grow
Into a better writer
I've always loved writing
And that's when I knew
This is what I'm supposed to do
Writing is my purpose
I started to love myself
I started to find who I am
I started to believe in myself
No...
I'm not always happy
But don't fucking piss on my parade
Because...
I literally had to fight
The demons that I was dancing with
The demons are still lurking
But now I know how to fight them
I needed my flashlight to find myself
To love myself finally
I'm quirky

I'm sarcastic
I'm caring
I'm a lone wolf
I'm a writer
I know who I am today
So don't ever try to take that away
You either can run with me
Or you either can lurk from the darkness
Either way...
I'm following this arrow
And I'm going to keep going forward
Never going back
Because...
Underneath this quirky soul
Is a fucking savage

Watercolor Sky

I love how the sunset caresses your cheek bones
As you lay there in the open range field of happiness
Looking at you with a big ole smile
You wrap your arm around my waist
And I run my fingers through your hair
As we just captivate the watercolor sky
That mother nature has gifted us
Seriously...
Is this what paradise supposed to feel like

The Phoenix In Me

Im literally taking this writing thing seriously
I swear I was NEVER good at anything else
But this passion of mine
People say I'm good at it
Some say I have a gift
So I'm putting this talent to use
I'm going to let these words
Inside this quirky soul & fucked up mind of mine
Grow like a fucking wildflowers
And...
When I take my last breath
I want the people who awakened
This phoenix soul inside me
And who believed in me & encouraged me
NOT cry for me
But...
Keep my ink that I bled on these sheets of paper
Inside your minds & hearts
Because...
I want my ashes & words burn together
Like a...
WILDFIRE
And..
The smoke to rise like a magnificent majestic
PHOENIX

Unique Roses & Vines

Admire her like she's fine art
Love her as if she'll slip through
Your fingers like hot summer sand
At any given second
Kiss her as if she is your oxygen
Plant gorgeous roses & vines
Inside that sturdy ribcage
So those beautiful butterflies & hummingbirds
Can fly high & free
Because...
Even if you look high & low
There isn't another like her

Spellbinding

I think if you stood
Right in front of me
I'd be a nervous reck
No...No...I'd definitely would
I'd capture every detail of your gorgeous face
Like I was a face recognition robot
I would want to slowly
Trace my fingertips over your kissable lips
I would want to kiss you
As if it was my last time kissing you
But...
I'd be hesitant as if I was in shock
So I would hope you'd kiss me first
My soul would get so lost
In your beautiful captivating eyes
That you would need a flashlight
You would have to search deep
In my ribcage to find those beautiful
Lilies that you planted with your love
I'd fall in love with you every single time
As my name dripped off your tongue
As it echoed off the walls
I think if you stood right in front of me
I'd melt like milk chocolate
That's swirled with English toffee

Bur(rrr)den

Walking along the dirt road
Pebbles skidding along
As the thorns & vines follow behind
Head down
Her shoulders are slumped
The tears of burden fall down her cheeks
Thinking...
"I'm a fucking burden"
"I'm fucking useless"
"Nobody needs me"
Moments later...
The vines start to crawl up her leg
Thorns ripping her pants
Looking down again
More tears fall down her face
Drip, Drop
Drip, Drop
They start to grow within her body
Looking down at her right palm
A dark japanese carmine rose bloomed
She wiped her tears with her other hand
Whispering....
"Gorgeous"

Kaleidoscope

My mind never slows down
I'm either worrying about things I can't control
Or thinking about what I'm going to write
I'm always looking at art
I love all forms of art
But...
I love abstract art the most
Black & white art is very captivating
The mind is a beautiful mysterious place
When you look at art
Or read someone's writing
Each person who looks at it or reads it
They see or imagine something different
And...
I find that so damn beautiful
I once told my best friend
That I have a vintage purple cabinet in my head
Which is full of characters & ideas
Honestly...
Is this how all writers & artists feel or think
Or is it just how my quirky mind works
Actually...
It kinda reminds me of
A vintage kaleidoscope

Nina: Her Fighting Shield

(Dedicated To My Little Sister)

The sky was black as coal. I was standing in the middle of a busy four way street. Cars passing me by like people loaded up their gas tanks with energy drinks.

Just standing still like my batteries wore out. I was wearing a lavender bandana, white T-shirt, white torn jeans, dark brown boots with lavender shoe laces.

Cars passing me by as if I wasn't even fucking standing there.

I feel a sudden heat wave behind me. I turned around fast. There it was seven feet tall, dark black pebble looking substance floating in front of me.

I looked the pebbles substance up & down. Then it swirled around me quickly. I closed my eyes, balled up my fingers into a fist. I stood in a strong stance, and screamed as loud as I could.

The pebbles formed a devilish smile, as it swirled around me again.

I could feel a hot electric wave in my soul. I opened my eyes, and I saw my sister standing in front of me. The electric wave left me, and I walked up to give her a hug. My arms went through her, I tried again, same fucking thing.

I saw the pebbles hover over my sister. I looked at her, and I saw a projection playing over her body. It was clips of us when we were younger, up until now. Then it went black. I walked up, and saw my reflection. My eyes were glowing lavender. I blinked several times, still lavender.

I stepped back. I felt tears running down my cheeks. I felt the electric wave in my soul again. My hands were in fists, I looked up at the pebbles still hovering over her. I belted out a scream, and my hands shot out an electric bolt towards the pebbles. It swerved to the left, but was still hovering over my sister.

Looking down at my hands, I saw tiny shock waves over my fingers.

Thinking...

Is this what true anger feels like?
I'm so angry...
I can't fix her, I can't fix her
She's my little sister, my best friend, my birthday twin
And I can't fucking fix her.

Balling my hands into fists again, I had anger in my soul. I blasted another electric bolt at the black piece of shit that was hovering over my sister. I couldn't destroy this thing.

My sister walked towards me, then circled around me. Then stood back in front of me. I felt more calm.

The wind blew around us, and I heard her voice

"You're so stubborn Ash...you know what to do"

The wind stopped, and she walked away

Falling to my knees, I just started balling. The pavement was cold. I wiped my tears, and looked up to the sky.

{{Screaming}}

"FUCK...."

I stood up, brushed off my knees, and just stood there with my head down. I felt defeated, I was angry, I was sad, I was tired...but I wasn't fucking done.

{{Whispering}}

"I need help, I need help, I can't do this myself"

As I stood there, I felt a hand on my shoulder. Another hand on my other shoulder. I felt their positive energy around me. I turned around and saw familiar faces. Some were whispering, some were on their knees praying, some just closed their eyes, some kissed their crosses on their necklaces. I looked up to the sky, and I saw messages floating in the sky.

I put my head down, and closed my eyes. Tears kept falling as I whispered positive thoughts and vibes, and prayers towards my sister's way.

The wind started blowing harder, and I heard my sister's voice.

"Now"

I stood in front of the pebbles form substance, put my hands in front of it, and I let out a lavender shield over my sister.

The pebbles formed a devilish smirk, and tried to penetrate the shield. My family, friends and familiar faces circled around the shield that was protecting my sister.

{{Shouting}}

"She's a fucking fighter, and we're fighting along beside her every step of the fucking way."

Biography

Asher Phoenix was born and raised in Illinois. She was born with a rare disability called Arthrogryposis Multiplex Congenita. She had her struggles, but they didn't stop her from living a "normal" life.

You'll notice that Asher is a quirky, sarcastic, and funny person with a big heart.

In her debut book, *Kaleidoscope*, Asher talks about mental health, love, and the struggles and triumphs of having a disability.

One of her favorite childhood memories is commuting from Illinois to her Michigan summer home with her family. Days were spent swimming, raft fighting, fishing, building bonfires, rock hunting, pontooning, and paddle boating.

She now resides in Michigan.

Instagram
@asher.phoenix_writes